Reticent

Reticent

Poems

Abby N. Lewis

Grateful Steps
Asheville, North Carolina

Acknowledgments

Many, many thanks to the following individuals who provided invaluable feedback and made a lasting impression on my writing: Sarah Eichelman, for both seeing and encouraging the potential in my work; Jodi Nicely and Steven Hodgin, for your kindness and tolerance in reading the scribbles of a frustrated, angst-filled teenager; the Department of Literature and Language faculty and staff at ETSU, for providing an academic environment in which my creativity thrived; Maggie Gregg, Timothy Davis, Matthew Gilbert, and many other early readers and supports of my creative endeavors; and Micki Cabaniss, for making this collection a reality.

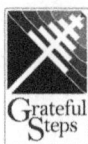

Grateful Steps Foundation
333A Merrimon Avenue
Asheville, North Carolina 28801

Library of Congress Control Number 2016944427
Lewis, Abby N.
Reticent

Illustrated by Chelsea Lewis

Variations of poems in this collection have appeared in the following publications: "My Time" in *Gallery* 2014. "Reticent," originally titled "Picturing God," in *Gallery* 2016. "The Essence of Lounging" in volume 7.2 of *Outrageous Fortune*.

ISBN 978-1-935130-88-8 Paperback

Printed in the United States of America
Lightning Source

FIRST EDITION

www.gratefulsteps.org

For my family, and the unwavering support you provide,
and for Eva Price, who always asks for a story

Stranger, if you passing meet me and desire to speak to me, why should you not speak to me?
And why should I not speak to you?

"To You"
- Walt Whitman

"The time has come," the Walrus said,
"To talk of many things:"

"The Walrus and the Carpenter"
- Lewis Carroll

Contents

Reticent

I.

II.

II.

IV.

Reticent

The stranger who lends an extra
five for diapers at the grocery store.

A mother kissing a boy's scraped
knee after a bicycle wreck.

On the side of the road, a man who
insists on feeding his dog before himself.

A nurse who turns on the television at five
sharp each day, knowing it soothes the patients.

The little boy who writes a note of appreciation
for his teacher, earning her a thousand dollars.

A patron who leaves a tip large
enough to pay the waiter's rent.

The young woman who smiles at the boy meandering past,
head down, hands shoved in blue cotton fabric, kicking stones.

I.

Vital Dance

In bed, listening to the metronome in my ear, the tiny timekeeper
who will not let me sleep, taking life with each beat into the drum,

    tap by tap, a Morse code message in a long-lost language.

Why do I sleep knowing that time will pass as I do so? I am free to dance
when Father Time is drowsy, lulled by the white coin in the sky, suspended

    between heads or tails. In those moments, we wait, hold

our breath, and dance together in familiarity from which we came and
shall return one day, when our knees are weak and our hair a color

    akin to the moon.

One two heads three four tails five six last seven eight day

    hush

A Delicate Gift

She unspools the
bow of the ribbon.
Her hands shake,
pulling it taut.
An accident.
It snaps at her,
nonetheless.
Then she eases her
finger under the tape,
cringes every time
she hears a tear—
A glance at
his face
and a soft smile.

Morsels from the Vine

The piercing scream of the wheel on the shopping cart makes the woman flinch as she pushes it over to the produce section. Her son giggles in the seat in front of her, his thin feet dancing through the holes of his cage. She picks up a bag of grapes and places it beside the boy. The sound of the zipped seal unzipping reverberates off the walls. She winces and glances around before reaching her hand into the opening. Pulling out a bundle, she moves the cart forward again, realizing she's been stationary for too long. She browses through the store, shelves lined with impossible temptations, feeding him grapes all the while. He arches his neck, a baby bird impatient for food that has already been devoured, blindly stealing it from his mother's stomach. When the bag is half empty, she parks the cart filled with miscellaneous items in a deserted aisle, folds her son to her chest, and flies from the scavenged lot.

The Fall of Eve

They stood together at the top of the stairs.
She gazed down the flight before them as if
to receive an attendant who would ask for
their tickets. He probed her mind, saw that
she was imagining a red apple falling down
the stairs, jagged slices and bruises opening
on the tender flesh. It rolled to rest at the base
of the descent. She wondered how long it would
take before someone cared to pick it up, if he
would throw it away or bring it close to his face
and breathe in the smell to determine its worth.
Perhaps he would place it where it could live out its
days watching the motion picture reel by as it turned
brown from the inside out, or maybe it would remain
in the vacant corner at the bottom, forgotten despite
its glorious fall—a trail of ants thirsty for its sweet tears
the only sign of a skirmish.

Circumspect

She walked with her toes pointed,
as if testing the waters of life
before every step she took.

Dr. Robert Peters

He pokes and prods his patients, tells
them what they don't want to hear.
Try to get out and exercise, he says.
Be active. A broken record. He asks a
three-hundred-pound man, *When was the last
time you cooked your own meal, from scratch?*
The man hems and haws and avoids the question,
lamenting how busy his life is, how difficult,
stressful. The doctor nods sympathetically, thinks
of the dishes piled in the sink at home, how she
never would have allowed such disarray.

He tells a young woman later that she should refrain
from using Q-tips to clean her ears for the rest of her
life. He ignores the frown, but notices a familiar stoop
in the shoulders. He signed a note excusing a boy who
had a "cold" from school that morning. The mother
hovered as the doctor wrote. Now he enters his office,
letting the nurse know he'll be with the next patient in
a few minutes. He opens a leaflet on his desk from the
funeral service yesterday, fingers the wedding ring beside it.
He glances up at the college diploma on his wall and sighs.

A Regulated Man

He laughed as if he'd lived his entire
life in a library, trained to contain that
impulsive explosion of joy. He managed
to shape something sudden and wild,
and she loved him for it.

The Proust Phenomenon

The pages wave at her as she
glances through the book. A few
over-exuberant leaves nip her nose
when she leans in. She scrunches up
her face with a laugh and touches a
finger to the injury. Pulling back, she
tsk-tsks, reprimanding the stray
spirits. She presses her nose as close
to the stitchings of the open novel as
she can, breathes in the familiar smell
of knowledge—crayon boxes and dusty
library shelves, the lingering vanilla
perfume of the previous owner.

Lying on her stomach at the beach,
legs crossed behind her, shiny from
the sunscreen bottle with the image
of the blond little girl, finger to cheek,
the mischievous brown dog intent on
making off with her blue bottoms.

Suspended between two trees
in a hammock at school, head
cradled in her arm, the open
book refracting the sunlight as
petals fall into the oversized net.

Sitting in the doctor's
office, bent almost double,
staring at the blurred words
in an attempt to suppress
the sounds around her.

The pages continue to rustle in
her hands, knowing they have
found a worthy reader—one who
seeks to pump life into the worlds
of the dead, placing an invisible
snapshot of her day like a bookmark
into the pages of every story she's
read, a scattered photo album.

Hyena Song

He follows behind as I walk past,
stalking like a hyena as I make my
way to another part of the hallway.
I sit on the floor as he stops, above
and behind me, stares blankly at a
$\qquad$ poster on the wall.

He accosts me with his nonsensical
laughter, monologuing to the air—
the kind of man who speaks in order
to be heard, no respect for the power
of words, the grace that comes with
$\qquad$ wielding them. I open a book.

Behind me, he pauses, glares at
the poster, hand on chin, begging
to be asked what he thinks. I ignore
my cue, let the moment pass. Yet still
he stands, waits until the sigh, the glance
$\qquad$ at him, and the song begins anew.

Nocturnal Auras

A blue trail of bright noctiluca in the
waves, river through the ocean.
Fireflies pulse in the fading light,
absorb the last rays of sun.
The candle flickers at the log cabin
window, conducted by invisible hands.
A lighthouse beam slices the dusk,
intent on an uninterrupted path.

The flashlight of the sky, forever
hunting for its elusive companion.

For the Angel Lady

Every time you came to the grocery store,
you gave the cashier a wire angel secured
with a ribbon, always a different color.

I was lucky enough to get two little
blessings—brown and yellow. They
hang from the black window curtain

in my room, looped around the
employee name badge. I never
bothered to learn your name.

When you stopped walking through
the door, I could ask no one where
you had gone. Instead, I fingered the

wire memories that rested across from
my heart and marveled at how something
so coarse could feel so smooth.

My Time

Shadows quiver on the wall
as the candle flickers, then
fizzles to nothing. The hands
creep along, comfortably
concealed within the night.
I know there is no hope left,
no chance of survival. All I
can do is close my eyes and
concentrate on my breath.

I shouldn't be this terrified.
They warned me he would
come. In my passion, I ignored
their incessant voices. And so I close
my eyes in dreaded anticipation as the
cold fingers tease their way up my spine
in their own twisted anticipation. Still,
I can't help but think, *It was worth it.*

Flashes

Thunder rocks the house, jolts me awake. From
the other room, I hear my sister jump out of bed.
In a moment, my door will open, and she will crawl
in beside me, wrap an arm around my waist, tell me
she is scared. I smile as another flash frames her
face in my doorway; I reach out a hand and pull her
under the covers with me, just like old times when
we shared a bunk bed. I was excited when Katie
moved out at eighteen because it meant I finally
got a room to myself, no more staring at the bowed
mattress above me. Chelsea used to wait until I was
settled before she would let one loose five feet from
my nostrils, then lean over the side rail and ask if I
could smell it yet. Other nights, we talked of things
we never mentioned during the day; how Mom and
Dad were yelling at each other more than they usually
did, that Katie's room smelled like cigarettes, whether
it was okay to still be a virgin at sixteen, if people could
tell. I rest my arm over hers and bring up the bunk bed
days. Another boom drowns out her reply, but her warm
breath on my hair tells me all I need to know.

II.

On "Identity"

Let them be as flowers,
always watered, fed, guarded, admired,
but harnessed to a pot of dirt.
                    —*Julio Noboa Polanco*

My sixth-grade English teacher points a finger at each of
us in turn, asks, "Would you rather be a flower or a weed?"

A chorus of flowers sets us off, but as the accusatory finger
moves closer, weeds begin to crop up in the familiar mouths

of classmates. When the finger of fate rests on me,
I stare at the weeds that came before and choose flower,

resolving to oppose the majority despite knowing my
answer is wrong in her eyes. Meadows filled with rolling

wildflowers that have felt no touch but the wind's can agree,
not every beauty is potted in a perfect circular home.

Feverish Delusions of a Walrus and a Carpenter

From scalp to sacrum and out,
the waves crash through me.

They chill the blood, immobilize the limbs. I close my
eyes and teeter in the chair, the vessel. At the front of the

room, the teacher talks of a play
while I focus on steering.

Another wave passes by, and I let out a slight moan, shift course
leeward. I rest my head momentarily on the hardwood desk, unsure

if I can weather this internal
storm. The last thing I think
is *why the sea is boiling hot.*

Picture of a Man

I could almost see him
with one of those pitchforks,
not a violent image, but more
akin to the classic picture of the
farmer and his wife. In that photo,
the man seems reserved. This man
looks more accepting. He's had that
pitchfork for years, and he knows he'll
never do anything else. He's seen the
power his weapon can yield, all the
work he could get done in a year.

But he lacks motivation, agency.
He does not care if his fingers
stiffen around the handle, molding
like clay to the instrument—
no longer an independent entity,
merely a farmer with a pitchfork.

Nothing but Words

But what does it mean?
a persistent peer asked.
She sat leaning forward
in her seat, as if she could
reach out a hand and pull
the answer from his mind
with nothing but brute
determination. His mouth
opened like a hidden tunnel
suddenly revealed before
blending back into the foliage.
He turned his gaze to the paper,
forcing himself to face the words
he had written on the page.

A Tasteful Home

In Dandridge, the olives taste black, as
the name suggests. They are dense and
split slowly, the seams opening around
the hole as I place them on my fingers,
always willing to play my alien game.

The ones in Johnson City are watery
and sour, with an aftertaste similar to
the oil. These will not fit on my fingers;
most are deflated, as if they know what
a disappointment they are. Asheville-grown

strawberries bring to mind the bruised
blackberries that sit in the bottom of a
basket, forgotten and smothered by the
weight of siblings, softened by too much
love. They taste nothing like home. There,

the strawberries are rich and voluptuous—
so red one would think the color had been
tampered with, and perhaps it had. As I sit
at the rickety table held aloft by one mediocre
leg and a few screws attached to the wall,

I smile over the fact that the taste
of local fruit is always the first
thing I miss in a new town; not
family, pets, the scenery, but
the reminiscent food of childhood.

Memories Ablaze

We stand side by side, silhouetted against
the night as the flames eat away at our
house. A cloud of smoke rises from the
dining room, forsaken distress call. With
every second that passes, another memory
disintegrates—a journal from my elementary
days, a stuffed Jack Russell Terrier my sister
got when she was three, a clock of Elvis whose
pelvis will no longer swing in tandem with the
time. She reaches out her hand for mine, but I
pull her to me and let the dampness seep into
the fabric of my cotton shirt as the wind weaves
ashes into my hair, a half-hearted apology.

Springboro, Ohio

-for Christina Bretz

The Dairy Queen on the corner of the street we
used to walk to during those sweltering summer
                 days, now a gutted-out shell.

The idle chatter that once filled the air, consumed
by muffler engines, sputtering trucks and blared horns.

A single tree in the front of the yard, which
held the little girl in its boughs, frozen in time.
          The porch swing rocks with the ghost of motion.

An empty marble tub that used to hold the sud-covered bodies
                 of gleeful children within its belly.

The plastic violin on a plastic pedestal,
         stray strings curled from neglect.

Walls lined with china plates of birds,
            a tremor away from clipped wings.

The neighbor's walkway, still choked
         with grape ivy, philodendron, spider plants.

Gnomes across the road, posed in mockery,
            rosy cheeks and gesturing hands.

An empty bunk bed, fit for two, dust
                  its only occupant.

23

Coccinellidae

I stare as you crawl along the shirt I tossed upon the bed that
morning, toothpick legs leaving an invisible trail of the potent
odor you emit like a skunk whenever my shadow falls across you.

This is not your house. Get out! I have catered to your needs
long enough. At first I was kind. I would return you to the
window whenever you wandered, coax you from the searing

embrace of the flower-shaped light near my bed. But it was
not long before I began to cringe at your presence. The way
you fluttered at the ceiling, bat out of hell. I stayed calm.

When you attacked I lost all coddling thoughts. You landed
on my cheek at midnight, intent on eating me, but the only
trace I could find of you on me was that ghastly smell. Now,

your corpses bob in the dirty dishes in my sink. You scuttle
along every wall, floor and ceiling, left and right. You are
even in my shoes, couch, and bed. You adorn my hair. I worry

that I will wake tomorrow and find you lining the inside of
my mouth, red inverted braces, sucking the soul from my body
with your needle feet. Next you will be in my food, and then
        what will the difference be between me and you?

Dear Grandpa Sawyer,

John caught a trout today—his first.
I watched from the top of the hill as
he reeled it in, and let me tell you,
that boy's sure got some strength in
him. I thought that fish was going to
pull him in for a swim instead of the
other way around. It was so huge he
had to drag it through the mud on the
bank, which squelched and sucked in
protest, refusing to relinquish one of its
prized children. I've got a picture that I'll
put in here. John says he wants you to frame
it and send him that dime you've promised him.

Yours,
Amelia Gene

The Essence of Lounging

Security is a kind of death.
—Tennessee Williams

She relishes the firmness
Of the soil against her back,
The pressure of gravity
Pinning her to the earth—
Like a fly caught in a web,
A solid part of terra firma.
Perhaps when she finally
Decides to rise, when the
Spider eventually comes,
Her body will have left an
Indentation—a memory
Of what has been.

Withering Willows

She sits quietly at her desk in class,
eyes downcast, pencil held loosely in her hands,
inevitably waiting for the time to take notes.
She does not realize that her mind
is already taking notes,
picking out the smallest details
in the conversations around her.
The way the brunette dominates the discussion
in the middle of the room,
the way the boys in the corner whisper,
sneaking sly glances at the long-haired,
straight-backed girls who vomit up
the word *like* ceaselessly as they speak.

She does not want to know what they think.

Her pencil rattles against her hand,
and her leg twitches nervously.
She slides lower in her seat and
glances around, searches the faces
of strangers, the stereotyped masks of society.

Her eyes meet another girl's in the back of the room.
A smile pulls at the corners of her mouth
and is returned.
Through the burning forest of faces,
she has found her willow tree.

Molded Earth

The way he softens his voice
when he speaks to her and no
one else, knowing others have
not offered the same courtesy.

A woman who smiles at each soul
she passes, even though she was
told it is a bad idea, that it
gives the wrong impression.

The boy who serenades the
girl on the swing set beside
him with his favorite love song.

The child who claims
the squirrel in the road
is not dead, only sleeping—

like the monster formed by piling people on people,
they bind together, become one solitary figure, alone
in the clay belly, open mouth filled with the dirty
soil of smothered deeds and staunched blood.

Time-lapse

I loved swimming as a child.
The way you would lap me up,
twirl me around and nudge me
back to the surface. You knew
I didn't belong there, but I gasped
a breath of air before sinking back
into your sun-kissed embrace,
oblivious to the danger.

Now you are angry with me.
You foam and seethe, and
even my salty tears betray me,
mingling with their brethren.
My body is mostly water.
You, the sea, know this—
I can feel you seeping through
my nose, my ears, my eyes, my eyes.

I am drowning in my own malleable
fluids, but I blame you, my childhood
friend. And I blame the moon, who
is so greedy to swallow me up.

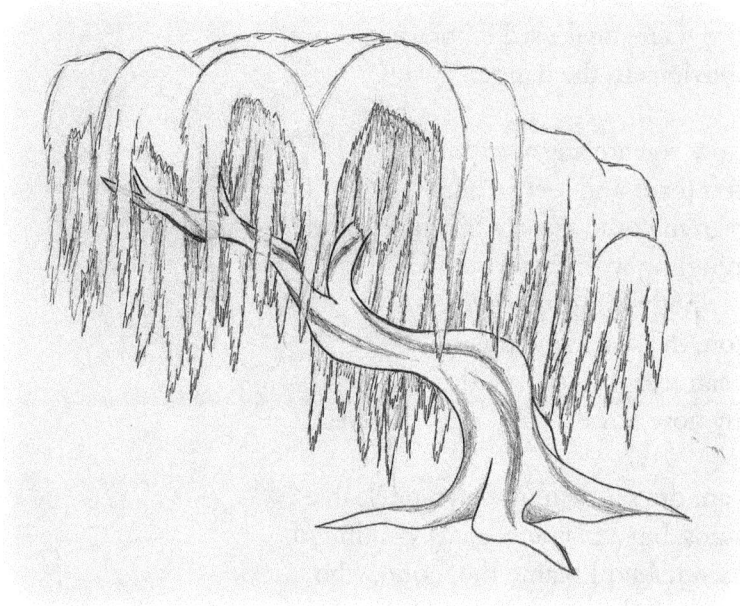

III.

The Art of Creation

A boy stands on a street corner in Paris,
watches the man across the way paint a
fresh view with each calculated stroke
of the brush. A wisp of a child observes
her grandmother as she weaves the story
of today into the tapestry. The young man
in the decrepit library of a college, the
sun illuminating the book in hand.

A dropped coin in an empty guitar case,
bodies at an art show. A photographer
who captures graffiti, displays it,
blue-thumbed amplification. Worn
records, converted VHS tapes, dusty
memories undusted by tender hands.

Fishing Lessons

I caught one, my sister says, reeling in the line. Her pole
curves toward the water, its spine arching like a frightened
cat's. The handle is snug against her hip, and the weight of
her body rests solely on her haunches as she leans back,
mirroring the pole. The line sings, moving faster than the eye
can catch, and the smooth surface of the water breaks, spits

a bass out of its dark maw, spattering the deck with flecks of
water and blood. She swings her pole first right, then left,
displaying her catch. Mother digs in the tackle box for the
pliers while my older sister and I gather around the victor,
congratulating her on a job well done, when the bass lets
out a shudder, releasing a waterfall of embryos onto the deck.

My sister and I jump backward, unsure what is happening.
She's just laid her eggs, says Mother. *She thinks she's going to die.*
We push the eggs into the water with our flip-flopped feet,
being as gentle as we can. We know they will not survive.
Mother unhooks the hollowed fish, tossing it back to the
depths. It lands with a resounding splash, taking with it all

our oxygen. Hunched in our lawn chairs on the deck,
staring at the dark spots on the wood where the eggs had
been, we turn our collective gaze out over Douglas Lake
from the edge of our grandparent's T-shaped dock.

Inked

He wasn't born with a book
in his hands—but his heart—and
every day the paper cut deeper
until someone noticed the blood
on his shirt. She gave him a quill
and said, "You must let the world
share in your sorrows. It will provide
the gauze and you the anesthesia."

The Scale of the World

I.

A round belly used to represent luck—
Now, jutting pelvises and collar bones
are how we judge our worth.

II.

Cattle dine more frequently than some
children, while other kids eat everything
in sight only to lie in bed loathing themselves.

III.

Sugar reigns from conveyor
belts while apples turn
soft on the shelf.

IV.

Chickens stare through mesh sunglasses
while the ignorant cries of a pig pierce the
air, trusting the man in the crimson boots
even as he opens a river on its neck.

Angel Food Cake

Hands sticky from the moist cake,
as soft as air, well worth the trudge
across the bridge and up the hill to
Grandma's house—the required
head bobbing fee of listening to her
talk of relatives in Ohio I've never
met. I also get a bag of trash to lug
to our house. Grandma can't afford
to pay the real trash man, but she
still places four silver quarters in
my hand, opposed to child labor
even after all these years.

The eating slows as I think of her,
trapped in her own home. She never
learned to drive, left her family to
follow her daughter, whose man had
the big idea to become an entrepreneur
in the second oldest town in Tennessee.
The cake lies heavy in my stomach,
feeling so different than it had in my
hands only moments ago. The only
remnants are sticky fingers that cling
to useless silver coins.

Sitting in the Grass

Sensing a slight tickle on my arm,
I glance down to find a small
Lime green bug crawling along.
It maneuvers through the hairs
As if through a field.
How odd it is that I am the
Giant, the soil, the path
This kiwi bug must trod.
He circles my thumb,
And as my shadow falls—
Enacting night—he
Continues, composed
Despite my presence.

Certified

I asked Mother once if my name had any
special origin, hoping for a grand story
that had to do with a long-dead relative
or perhaps a brave fictional character.

All she said, with a shrug of apology,
was, *No, I just liked the sound of it.*
I guess that means I'll have to compose
my own story—begin with the A—a

fitting letter. Transition into the stutter
of the double Bs. Next is the Y that always
comes too soon. What of all the letters
hidden in the crevices? Mother said she

named me what she did instead of Abigale
because she knew she and others would shorten
it, so why condemn me to a life of correcting
teachers and friends, demanding a name that

was not mine by right? Grandmother disagreed.
She claimed it was not proper, that Mother
was just being lazy. Now, when people become
familiar in my company, they switch to Abigale,

a backfired attempt at intimacy.
Gently, I inform them the condensed
version is in fact the only version, as
written on the birth certificate.

Waiting for the Dead

Her frail eyes scan the paper.
Another day, another list. A
shaky finger traces the words
on the page, praying that she
won't see a familiar name,
familiar face.
Her finger reaches the last
black dot, hovering over the
space above it before lowering
it delicately to rest upon the ink.

She bows her head, and the
newspaper mimics the action
as she releases all of the air she
had held captive as she read.
No one she knows today.
She'll check again tomorrow.

The Influence of Brian Crain

She sits on the inky couch,
cross-legged and hunched
over, struggling to make the
words flow. She pauses, becomes
aware of the stifling silence. With
a laugh, she reaches for her phone.
The "Butterfly Waltz" begins to emit
from the depths of the device, and
the cogs whirl into motion. Like the
dancer in a music box, she cannot
function without the accompanying
tune. Her hands glide over the keyboard,
transform into peach flats, ribbons laced
up the legs of her fingers. Together they
work to translate the music into images,
the images to ideas, ideas to words,
and words to a story—the story of the
hunchbacked ballerina.

Decrepit Motor Home

I stand in the small shower,
Victorian wallpaper to my
right, a plastic guard rail and
curtain that blocks nothing, not
even the water, which seeps
beneath the uneven gap between
it and the tub, to my left.

Lukewarm water teases
me for a moment before
switching to ice that drags
the shudders from my
vulnerable body.

A spider decides this is the
opportune moment to introduce
himself. He hangs from the bar,
retreats whenever I straighten.

I exit the space feeling more soiled
than when I entered. The oils from
the conditioner cling to the tangled
locks at the back of my head.

Opening the door, I leave one small
space only to enter another, slightly
larger—a fun house mirror room that
throws unsightly parts of my body
back at me from every angle.

I wrap myself in the cerulean beach
towel; the whites of my knuckles
holding the fabric in place reflect
across each mirror, one final taunt
before our next scheduled encounter.

Ascent to Pandemonium

The breath clings to my windpipe, scraping
its way up and out of my esophagus.

There is a demon in my throat, acting up
every time I attempt to swallow.

He expands to block the air
from entering the lungs.

I attack his house, a feeble
tornado, but he is in the eye,

calm in the midst of my storm.
This is the worst sickness of all.

I climb to the top of the stairs,
force my body into overexertion,

my heart beating *you are fine
you are fine* into my head.

INursery Rhyme

For the most part, the poem
runs free on the page, but
every once in a while, there
is a childish interruption—
look at me, look at me!
I am special.

Although childish, it has
the power of an anchor; it
grounds attention to the
familiar, arrests the harsh
world—reminding us of fairies
and people who live in oversized
shoes—glass slippers, golden hair,

symbols of hope, dreams. Is not the
world but an illusion, mundane
interposed with the occasional
sighting of reality, magic?
The empty crib sways in answer.

Master of the Galaxy

A basketball player, tossing and spinning
the planets in the air, twirling, throwing them
above his head, behind his back. He rotates
one on a single finger, pulls it close and
slows it down for a
moment,
suspending time.

He smiles, runs a finger along one of the lines—
black ribbon racing across the world. He pulls back,
resumes his circus act,
spinning and tossing and twirling and risking it all—
a single ball,
sphere of orange and black.

IV.

Ode to Raymond

She is in the shower when
the song comes on. She
reaches out for the white wall,
shoulder against the wet plastic,
the palm of one hand pressed to
starkness, reaching for the ocher
face that is no longer there.

The noises escape her lips,
and she is grateful for the
waterfall above her head,
pounding the sounds against
the ground of the tub. The
words of the singer circle
her mind with memories.

She sinks to the floor,
arms pulling bare legs to
chest as the steam rises
to obscure her outline.

The System

I.

I show up thirty minutes late for the exam,
hair shoved into a messy bun, stray curls
escaping the embrace of the black hair tie.

I grab a scantron and number two pencil at
the door, then walk up and accept the test
from the teacher's outstretched hand, eyes

lowered to avoid his. Finding a seat, I stare
at the paper. The teacher makes his way to
me, rests one hand on the back of my chair,

the other splayed on the table. He leans close
and whispers that he'll give me an A if I make
a ninety, no questions asked. All I can think is

that I have not showered in days, wonder if
he can tell. The coating of fuzz on my teeth from
a mixture of coffee, glazed donuts and neglect

pulses in disgust at my sympathy-worthy
appearance. I glance at his face, etched with
past hardships—all the years he has lived

without his wife, the bed that is too big.
A thanks makes its way from my mouth
as I bow to the task ahead, filling empty

circles with dark gray lead. He returns
to the front of the classroom, confident
in his stab at motivating a student.

II.

86—the number that stares up at
me after careful calculations.

Around me, fellow students are
altering the past with frantic

scribbles built on lies. I do
not possess the same reckless

nature, although I feel
the urgency as much as

they do. Two symbols
represent a third—a letter,

which determines three numbers
interrupted with a single dot

after the first that will predict
the amount of still more virtual

symbols that I will receive in
the form of collateral for being

a *promising student*. Resisting the
urge to cave to the twitch in my

fingers, I let my pencil clatter to
the table and hand the teacher the

paper with my future on it.
He glances at it, then wraps

an arm around my shoulder,
presses me to his side, and

plants a sloppy kiss on my
forehead. He tells me, *you'll*

be fine. He was right—between
his hands and the official records,

the numbers changed. He told me that day
to make sure I come back and see him.

                                              I never have.

Concrete Ardor

At an art gallery, she'll talk of random objects and
images she sees in the abstract paintings, like animals
in the sky. Can you see them? she points. On a hiking
trail in Asheville, one of the ones with sign posts that read
this tree used to be carved by American Indians to make
spoons, this one bowls. She skips from one post to the next,
leans forward with her hands clasped behind her back,
bouncing excitedly on her heels all the while.

Somewhere you can watch her eyes go wide in
wonder as she takes in all the miracles of life around her—
like a newborn baby who is now old enough to see the
world beyond her mother's smiling face for the first time.

Gateway Gratification

I smoked Kings candy cigarettes as a child,
holding the chalk-like stick between two
      fingers, an imitation of success.

I ate bright powder off a white stick and drank
sparkling juice from a wine bottle, learning
      to crave the feeling of glass against my lips.

As a young adult, I bought placebo
drugs in a clear container, relishing
      their chatter in my mouth.

I chewed pseudo tobacco made from livestock,
a permanent circular crease in the pocket of my
      jeans, the illusion of greatness.

I was given the tools of destruction
before I could even spell the word.
      Now I have to learn bigger words.

Waning

In the summer time, Mother would lie
on the back deck for hours,
    breed freckles on her arms.

When she finally returned to the shade,
I stared at the stranger
    who called herself my life giver.

Grandmother, too, had unusual freckles—
one in particular resembled
    the sliver of a moon. I imagined

I was the wolf, come to howl over how
she never seemed to give
    my words any merit.

I stared at the thumb-nail sized silent
judge on her forearm in every conversation,
    never receiving an answer.

Now, Mother's freckles bleed together
like wax from melted crayons, and
    I work to separate one

from the others, searching for that absent
sliver in my life, the moon
    that was never full enough.

Golden Droplet

He noticed it in her hair one day
as they were talking in the empty
hall. He pointed it out, a yellow
contrast in the auburn, like fall.

She had blushed and untangled
it from the smooth curtain, thanked
him for noticing. He smiled as
she glanced around for a trash

can and presented his hand, said
he would throw it away for her.
Holding the flower between two
fingers, she dropped it into his palm.

He remembered being disappointed
that her hand hadn't brushed his.
When she wasn't looking, he placed
the bright blossom in his pocket.

It sits on his window sill,
now a dry, colorless husk.

Base Hospital Nurse

You swathe me in blankets,
bring biscuits and corned beef,
rest a cold rag on my forehead,
and check regularly to make
sure it's still damp.

You sit by the bed, and
we talk of nothing as
you exhume the toxins
from me, draw them
into you through the
movement of your
hands, your voice—
a gentle general who
has yet to lose a soldier.

Counterfeit Manifestation

I hand you the paper, the mask
of indifference daintily, yet
securely smoothed over my face.

My eyes watch yours as
they skim over the words,
lips moving silently as you
take them in. You finish,
give a curt nod, return it to
my hands and say, "It's good."

Those words—so simple—
so often spoken, become
the universe in an instant,
but the mask is firmly in place.

Desert Lake

I walk down past the edge of the grass—past
The drop off into the sudden desert to rest
Cautiously on the crumbling bricks that used
To make up one of the four walls of this home.

I close my eyes, try to imagine the life of its
Former residents. Every time, floating forms
Attack my lids, bang against the corners, springing
From one end to the other like acrobats, ridiculous

With their trailing bubbles, trapped air clinging to
Trapped flesh, wild animals caught in the serrated
Edges of my eyelashes. Why can't they be calm?
It would make the dying easier to watch.

Instead, they churn the air before me, force
Water out of my eyes and onto the dry sand
At my feet. Black starfish grow, stretch their
Limbs in the barren dust before retreating inward.

I-40 Westbound, North Carolina

Traffic slows to a crawl on the highway. Inconvenienced by the pile up,

I cut in front of a semi,

confident in my vehicle's small size. Luckily, my exit is just ahead. As

the engine climbs the hill,

I catch a glimpse of red lights surrounding a milky truck in the grass,

facing me. Shards of glass

from the vision pierce my retinas. The sounds of the radio, and my voice

aiding the singer's, are whipped away,

like the passenger's breath upon impact. A fog of guilt drops over the

shattered day, and rain begins

to fall, Nature's first step in cleansing the discolored flesh of the earth.

Sown Woman

She keeps all her secrets
hidden inside like a bouquet,
and when someone inquires
about her heart, she will
gladly give an easter lily
imprinted with the name
of her childhood friend,
a daisy deflowered by
all that could have been—
a dandelion that carries with it
all the wishes she has ever made.
And little by little
her bouquet will dwindle.
Although she will
be lost to the wind,
she will have spread her
garden of memories
across as many lifetimes
as there are seeds
in a pomegranate.

Downpour of Youth

She shifts her weight on the mattress,
thinks of the house that is her body. It's
old and rusty, no longer as sleek and polished
as it once was. Her skin is cracked and flaking
like the bark of a sycamore; some spots are white,
others are dark, colored with blossoming bruises
born from the air. They spread over her veins,
creep up the walls of her house.

An idea comes to her, and she plants
her feet on the floor, shuffles to the
door. *Silly girl,* she says to herself,
plants grow old and die when they go
too long without water. She unbolts the
wood and moves out into the storm. The
rain drums against her and she laughs, tilts
her head toward the sky to catch the rejuvenating
drops in the crevices of her face, the basin for the elixir.

Uprooted

Bees climb blindly into my cocoon,
confused by this man-made thing that
does not belong, a horizontal tree
that opens and closes, foreign Venus flytrap.

I wriggle in the depths, adjust my shape,
press my face against the fibers. They
leave no marks on me, yet I still feel the
imprint long after I've packed up and left.

I hold hands with the willow, run my
fingers through those of my savior,
thanking the being that keeps me
from falling to the ground.

Ants crawl over my sandaled feet
while the wind pulls the hand from
mine; we drop our branches, allow
gravity to separate us once again.